A Hundred and One Uses of a

DEAD·CAT

SIMON BOND

A HUNDRED AND ONE USES OF A DEAD CAT

First published in paperback in 1981 by Eyre Methuen Ltd
Published in a Mandarin paperback edition in 1991
This edition published in 2006 by Methuen & Co Ltd

1 3 5 7 9 10 8 6 4 2

Methuen & Co Limited
11–12 Buckingham Gate
London
SW1E 6LB

ISBN 10 digit: 0-413-77616-6
ISBN 13 digit: 978-0-413-77616-7

A CIP catalogue record for this title is available from the British Library

Printed in Great Britain by
St Edmundsbury Press Ltd, Bury St Edmunds, Suffolk

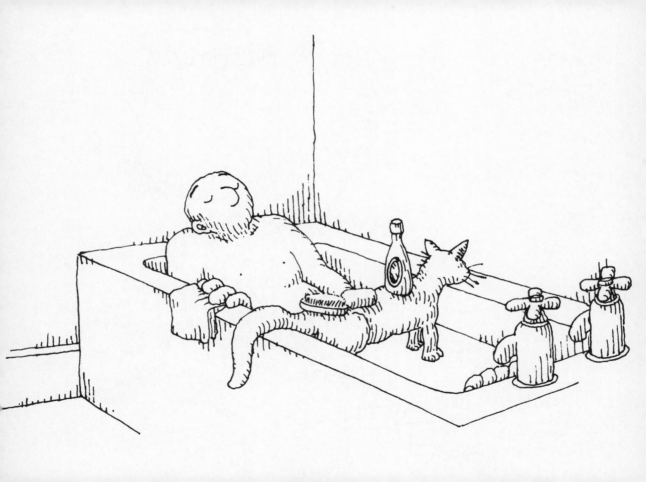

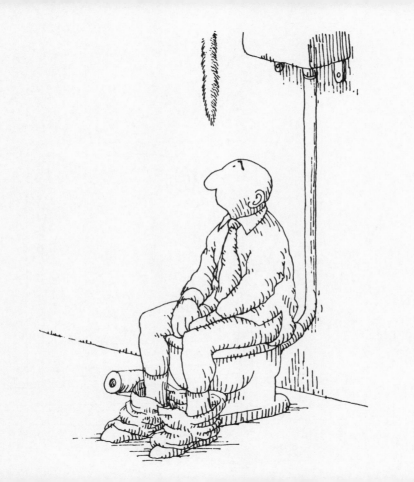

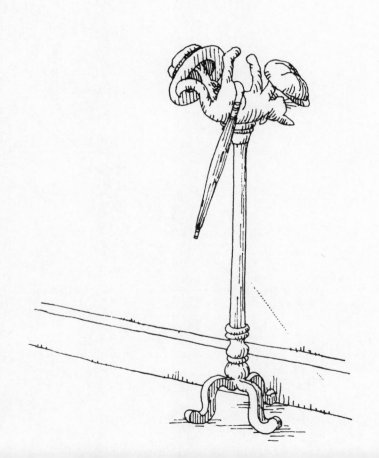

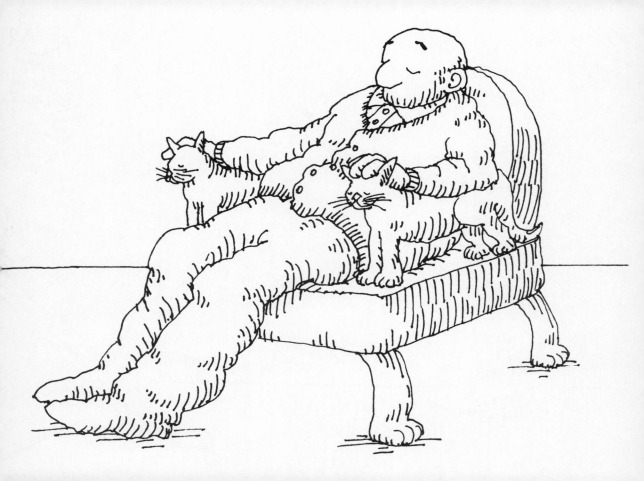

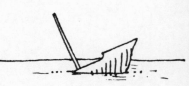

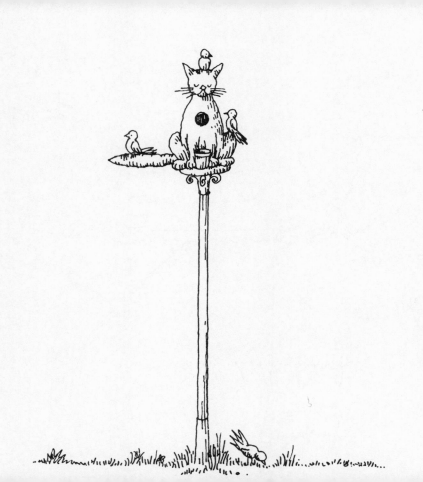

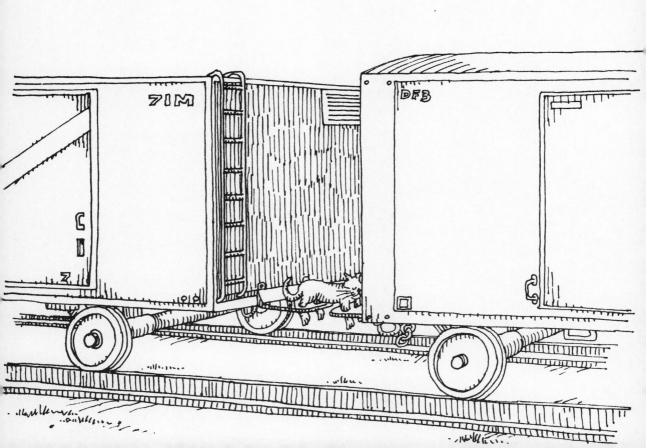

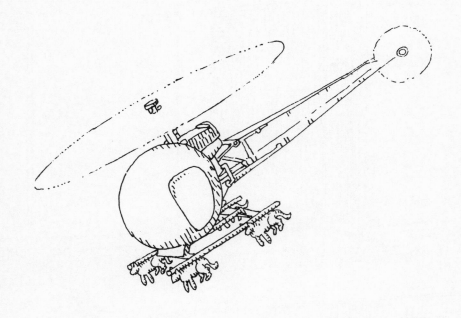

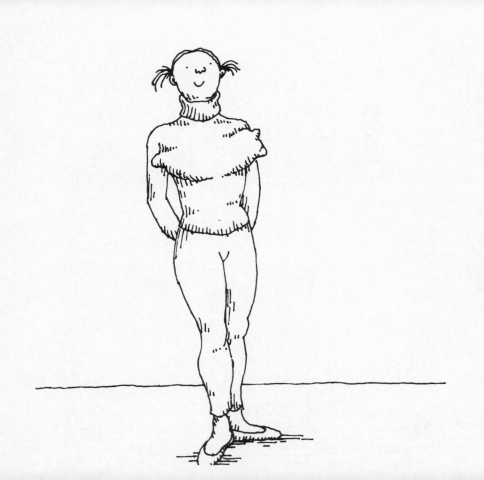

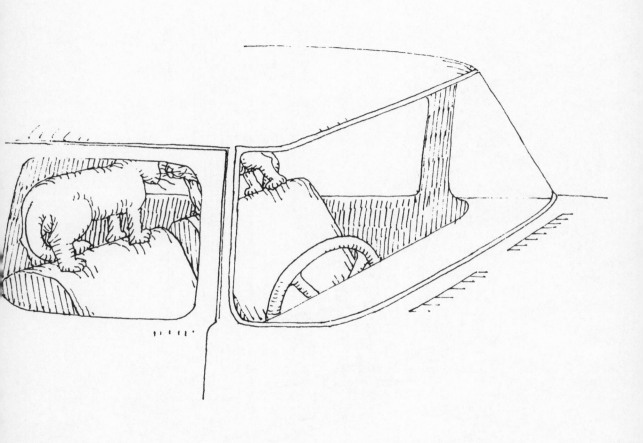

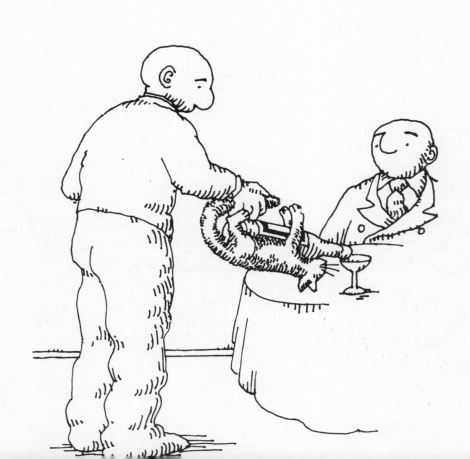

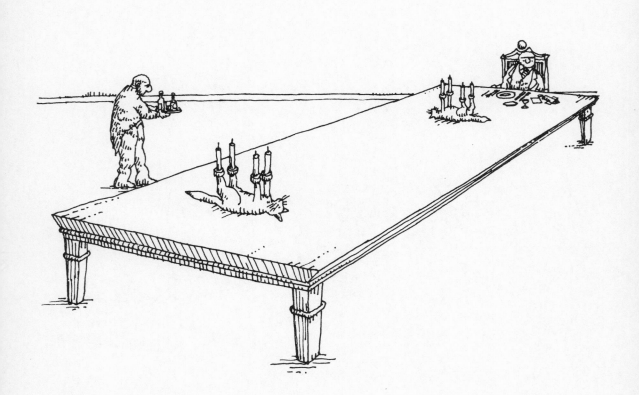

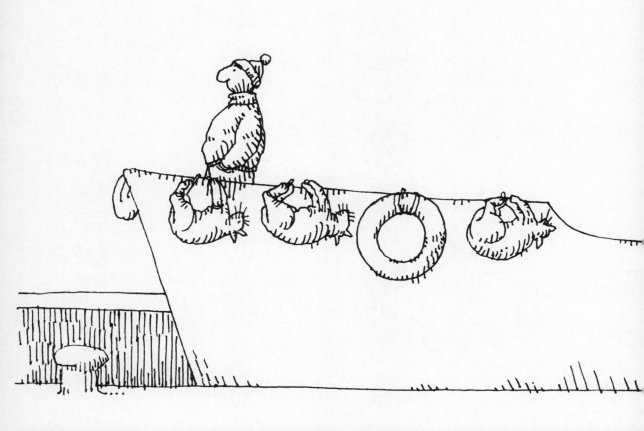

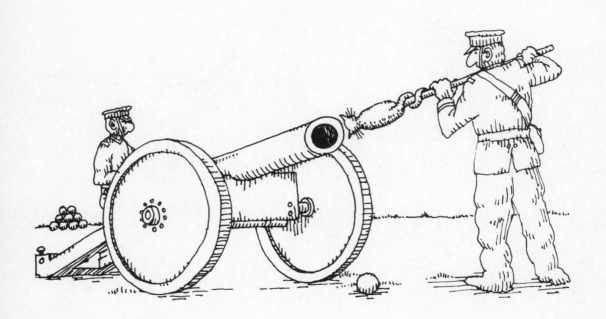

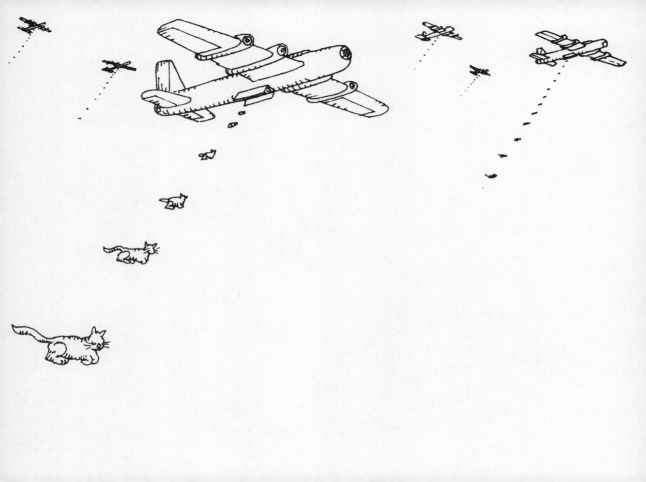

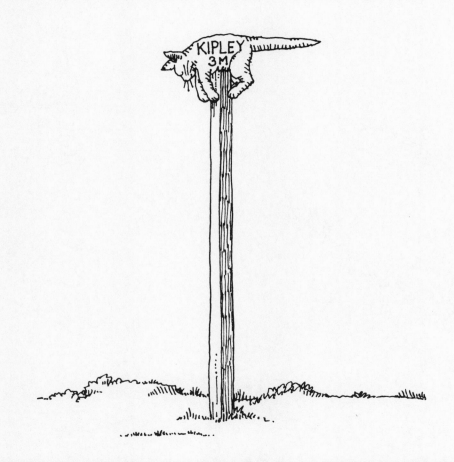

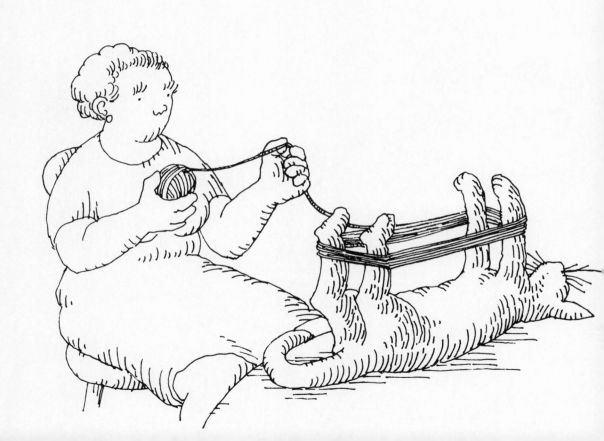

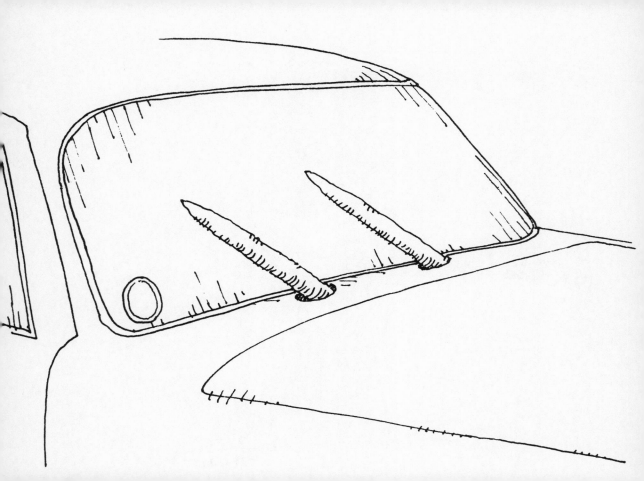

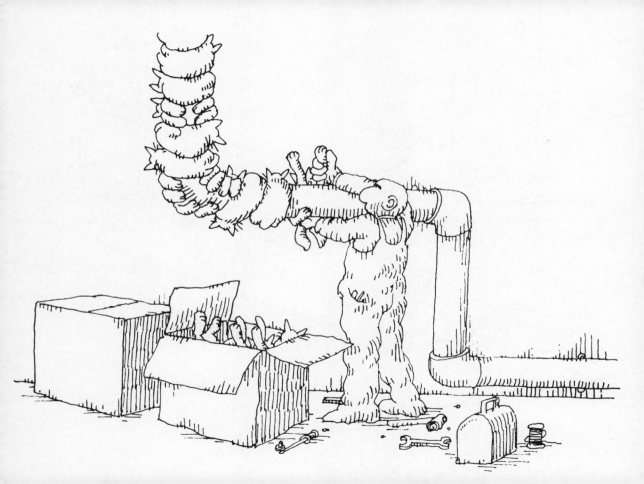

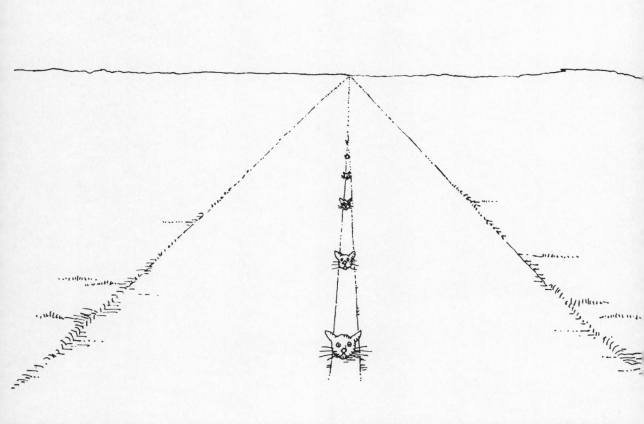